Confucius

CONFUCIUS

THE GREAT LEARNING

THE BIG NEST

THE BIG NEST

LONDON · NEW YORK · TORONTO · SAO PAULO · MOSCOW
PARIS · MADRID · BERLIN · ROME · MEXICO CITY · MUMBAI · SEOUL · DOHA
TOKYO · SYDNEY · CAPE TOWN · AUCKLAND · BEIJING

New Edition

Published by The Big Nest

This Edition first published in 2018

Copyright © 2018 The Big Nest

All Rights Reserved.

ISBN: 9781787247178

CONTENTS

THE GREAT LEARNING   7

THE GREAT LEARNING

What the great learning teaches, is to illustrate illustrious virtue; to renovate the people; and to rest in the highest excellence.

The point where to rest being known, the object of pursuit is then determined; and, that being determined, a calm unperturbedness may be attained to. To that calmness there will succeed a tranquil repose. In that repose there may be careful deliberation, and that deliberation will be followed by the attainment of the desired end.

Things have their root and their branches. Affairs have their end and their beginning. To know what is first and what is last will lead near to what is taught in the Great Learning.

The ancients who wished to illustrate illustrious virtue throughout the kingdom, first ordered well their own states. Wishing to order well their states, they first regulated their families. Wishing to regulate their families, they first cultivated their persons. Wishing to cultivate their persons, they first rectified their hearts. Wishing to rectify their hearts, they first sought to be sincere in their thoughts. Wishing to be sincere in their thoughts, they first extended to the utmost their knowledge. Such extension of knowledge lay in the investigation of things.

Things being investigated, knowledge became complete. Their knowledge being complete, their thoughts were sincere. Their thoughts being sincere, their hearts were then rectified. Their hearts being rectified, their persons were cultivated. Their persons being cultivated, their families were regulated. Their families being regulated, their states were rightly governed. Their states being rightly governed, the whole kingdom was made tranquil and happy.

From the Son of Heaven down to the mass of the people, all must consider the cultivation of the person the root of everything besides.

It cannot be, when the root is neglected, that what should spring from it will be well ordered. It never has been the case that what was of great importance has been slightly cared for, and, at the same time, that what was of slight importance has been greatly cared for.

Commentary of the philosopher Tsang

In the Announcement to K'ang, it is said, "He was able to make his virtue illustrious."

In the Tai Chia, it is said, "He contemplated and studied the illustrious decrees of Heaven."

In the Canon of the emperor (Yao), it is said, "He was able to make illustrious his lofty virtue."

These passages all show how those sovereigns made themselves illustrious.

On the bathing tub of T'ang, the following words were engraved: "If you can one day renovate yourself, do so from day to day. Yea, let there be daily renovation."

In the Announcement to K'ang, it is said, "To stir up the new people."

In the Book of Poetry, it is said, "Although Chau was an ancient state the ordinance which lighted on it was new."

Therefore, the superior man in everything uses his utmost endeavors.
In the Book of Poetry, it is said, "The royal domain of a thousand li is where the people rest."

In the Book of Poetry, it is said, "The twittering yellow bird rests on a corner of the mound." The Master said, "When it rests, it knows where to rest. Is it possible that a man should not be equal to this bird?"

In the Book of Poetry, it is said, "Profound was King Wan. With how bright and unceasing a feeling of reverence did he regard his resting places!" As a sovereign, he rested in benevolence. As a minister, he rested in reverence. As a son, he rested in filial piety. As a father, he rested in kindness. In communication with his subjects, he rested in good faith.

In the Book of Poetry, it is said, "Look at that winding course of the Ch'i, with the green bamboos so luxuriant! Here is our elegant and accomplished prince! As we cut and then file; as we chisel and then grind: so has he cultivated himself. How grave is he and dignified! How majestic and distinguished! Our elegant and accomplished prince never can be forgotten." That expression-"As we cut and then file," the work of learning. "As we chisel and then grind," indicates that of self-culture. "How grave is he and dignified!" indicates the feeling of cautious reverence. "How commanding and distinguished! indicates an awe-inspiring deportment. "Our elegant and accomplished prince never can be forgotten," indicates how, when virtue is complete and excellence extreme, the people cannot forget them.

In the Book of Poetry, it is said, "Ah! the former kings are not forgotten." Future princes deem worthy what they deemed worthy, and love what they loved. The common people delight in what delighted them, and are benefited by their beneficial arrangements. It is on this account that the former kings, after they have quitted the world, are not forgotten.

The Master said, "In hearing litigations, I am like any other body. What is necessary is to cause the people to have no litigations." So, those who are devoid of principle find it impossible to carry out their speeches, and a great awe would be struck into men's minds;-this is called knowing the root.

This is called knowing the root. This is called the perfecting of knowledge.

What is meant by "making the thoughts sincere." is the allowing no self-deception, as when we hate a bad smell, and as when we love what is beautiful. This is called self-enjoyment. Therefore, the superior man must be watchful over himself when he is alone.

There is no evil to which the mean man, dwelling retired, will not proceed, but when he sees a superior man, he instantly tries to disguise himself, concealing his evil, and displaying what is good. The other beholds him, as if he saw his heart and reins;-of what use is his disguise? This is an instance of the saying -"What truly is within will be manifested without." Therefore, the superior man must be watchful over himself when he is alone.

The disciple Tsang said, "What ten eyes behold, what ten hands point to, is to be regarded with reverence!"

Riches adorn a house, and virtue adorns the person. The mind is expanded, and the body is at ease. Therefore, the superior man must make his thoughts sincere.

What is meant by, "The cultivation of the person depends on rectifying the mind may be thus illustrated:-If a man be under the influence of passion he will be incorrect in his conduct. He will be the same, if he is under the influence of terror, or under the influence of fond regard, or under that of sorrow and distress.

When the mind is not present, we look and do not see; we hear and do not understand; we eat and do not know the taste of what we eat.

This is what is meant by saying that the cultivation of the person depends on the rectifying of the mind.

What is meant by "The regulation of one's family depends on the cultivation of his person is this:-men are partial where they feel affection and love; partial where they despise and dislike;

partial where they stand in awe and reverence; partial where they feel sorrow and compassion; partial where they are arrogant and rude. Thus it is that there are few men in the world who love and at the same time know the bad qualities of the object of their love, or who hate and yet know the excellences of the object of their hatred.

Hence it is said, in the common adage,"A man does not know the wickedness of his son; he does not know the richness of his growing corn."

This is what is meant by saying that if the person be not cultivated, a man cannot regulate his family.

What is meant by "In order rightly to govern the state, it is necessary first to regulate the family," is this:-It is not possible for one to teach others, while he cannot teach his own family. Therefore, the ruler, without going beyond his family, completes the lessons for the state. There is filial piety:-therewith the. sovereign should be served. There is fraternal submission:-therewith elders and superiors should be served. There is kindness:-therewith the multitude should be treated.

In the Announcement to K'ang, it is said, "Act as if you were watching over an infant." If a mother is really anxious about it, though she may not hit exactly the wants of her infant, she will not be far from doing so. There never has been a girl who learned to bring up a child, that she might afterwards marry.

From the loving example of one family a whole state becomes loving, and from its courtesies the whole state becomes courteous while, from the ambition and perverseness of the One man, the whole state may be led to rebellious disorder;-such is the nature of the influence. This verifies the saying, "Affairs may be ruined by a single sentence; a kingdom may be settled by its One man."

Yao and Shun led on the kingdom with benevolence and the people followed them. Chieh and Chau led on the kingdom with violence, and people followed them. The orders which these issued were contrary to the practices which they loved, and so the people did not follow them. On this account, the ruler must himself be possessed of the good qualities, and then he may require them in the people. He must not have the bad qualities in himself, and then he may require that they shall not be in the people. Never has there been a man, who, not having reference to his own character and wishes in dealing with others, was able effectually to instruct them.

Thus we see how the government of the state depends on the regulation of the family.

In the Book of Poetry, it is said, "That peach tree, so delicate and elegant! How luxuriant is its foliage! This girl is going to her husband's house. She will rightly order her household." Let the household be rightly ordered, and then the people of the state may be taught.

In the Book of Poetry, it is said, "They can discharge their duties to their elder brothers. They can discharge their duties to their younger brothers." Let the ruler discharge his duties to his elder and younger brothers, and then he may teach the people of the state.

In the Book of Poetry, it is said, "In his deportment there is nothing wrong; he rectifies all the people of the state." Yes; when the ruler, as a father, a son, and a brother, is a model, then the people imitate him.

This is what is meant by saying, "The government of his kingdom depends on his regulation of the family."

What is meant by "The making the whole kingdom peaceful and happy depends on the government of his state," this:-When the sovereign behaves to his aged, as the aged should be behaved to, the people become final; when the sovereign behaves to his elders, as the elders should be behaved to, the people learn brotherly submission; when the sovereign treats compassionately the young and helpless, the people do the same. Thus the ruler has a principle with which, as with a measuring square, he may regulate his conduct.

What a man dislikes in his superiors, let him not display in the treatment of his inferiors; what he dislikes in inferiors, let him not display in the service of his superiors; what he hates in those who are before him, let him not therewith precede those who are behind him; what he hates in those who are behind him, let him not bestow on the left; what he hates to receive on the left, let him not bestow on the right:-this is what is called "The principle with which, as with a measuring square, to regulate one's conduct."

In the Book of Poetry, it is said, "How much to be rejoiced in are these princes, the parents of the people!" When a prince loves what the people love, and hates what the people hate, then is he what is called the parent of the people.

In the Book of Poetry, it is said, "Lofty is that southern hill, with its rugged masses of rocks! Greatly distinguished are you, O grand-teacher Yin, the people all look up to you. "Rulers of states may not neglect to be careful. If they deviate to a mean selfishness, they will be a disgrace in the kingdom.

In the Book of Poetry, it is said, "Before the sovereigns of the Yin dynasty had lost the hearts of the people, they could appear before God. Take warning from the house of Yin. The great decree is not easily preserved." This shows that, by gaining the people, the kingdom is gained, and, by losing the people, the kingdom is lost.

On this account, the ruler will first take pains about his own virtue. Possessing virtue will give him the people. Possessing the people will give the territory. Possessing the territory will give him its wealth. Possessing the wealth, he will have resources for expenditure.

Virtue is the root; wealth is the result.
If he make the root his secondary object, and the result his primary, he will only wrangle with his people, and teach them rapine.

Hence, the accumulation of wealth is the way to scatter the people; and the letting it be scattered among them is the way to collect the people.

And hence, the ruler's words going forth contrary to right, will come back to him in the same way, and wealth, gotten by improper ways, will take its departure by the same.

In the Announcement to K'ang, it is said, "The decree indeed may not always rest on us"; that is, goodness obtains the decree, and the want of goodness loses it.

In the Book of Ch'u, it is said, "The kingdom of Ch'u does not consider that to be valuable. It values, instead, its good men."

Duke Wan's uncle, Fan, said, "Our fugitive does not account that to be precious. What he considers precious is the affection due to his parent."

In the Declaration of the Duke of Ch'in, it is said, "Let me have but one minister, plain and sincere, not pretending to other abilities, but with a simple, upright, mind; and possessed of generosity, regarding the talents of others as though he himself possessed them, and, where he finds accomplished and perspicacious men, loving them in his heart more than his mouth expresses, and really showing himself able to bear them and employ them:-such a minister will be able to preserve my sons and grandsons and black-haired people, and benefits likewise to the kingdom may well be looked for from him. But if it be his character, when he finds men of ability, to be jealous and hate them; and, when he finds accomplished and perspicacious men, to oppose them and not allow their advancement, showing himself really not able to bear them: such a minister will not be able to protect my sons and grandsons and people; and may he not also be pronounced dangerous to the state?"

It is only the truly virtuous man who can send away such a man and banish him, driving him out among the barbarous tribes around, determined not to dwell along with him in the

Auddle Kingdom. This is in accordance with the saying, "It is only the truly virtuous man who can love or who can hate others."

To see men of worth and not be able to raise them to office; to raise them to office, but not to do so quickly:-this is disrespectful. To see bad men and not be able to remove them; to remove them, but not to do so to a distance:-this is weakness.

To love those whom men hate, and to hate those whom men love;-this is to outrage the natural feeling of men. Calamities cannot fail to come down on him who does so.

Thus we see that the sovereign has a great course to pursue. He must show entire self-devotion and sincerity to attain it, and by pride and extravagance he will fail of it.

There is a great course also for the production of wealth. Let the producers be many and the consumers few. Let there be activity in the production, and economy in the expenditure. Then the wealth will always be sufficient.

The virtuous ruler, by means of his wealth, makes himself more distinguished. The vicious ruler accumulates wealth, at the expense of his life.

Never has there been a case of the sovereign loving benevolence, and the people not loving righteousness. Never has there been a case where the people have loved righteousness, and the affairs of the sovereign have not been carried to completion. And never has there been a case where the wealth in such a state, collected in the treasuries and arsenals, did not continue in the sovereign's possession.

The officer Mang Hsien said, "He who keeps horses and a carriage does not look after fowls and pigs. The family which keeps its stores of ice does not rear cattle or sheep. So, the house which possesses a hundred chariots should not keep a minister to look out for imposts that he may lay them on the people. Than to have such a minister, it were better for that house to have one who should rob it of its revenues." This is in accordance with the saying:-"In a state, pecuniary gain is not to be considered to be prosperity, but its prosperity will be found in righteousness."

When he who presides over a state or a family makes his revenues his chief business, he must be under the influence of some small, mean man. He may consider this man to be good; but when such a person is employed in the administration of a state or family, calamities from Heaven, and injuries from men, will befall it together, and, though a good man may take his place, he will not be able to remedy the evil. This illustrates again the saying, "In a state, gain is not to be considered prosperity, but its prosperity will be found in righteousness."

THE END

www.ingramcontent.com/pod-product-compliance
Lightning Source LLC
Chambersburg PA
CBHW021950160426
43195CB00011B/1308